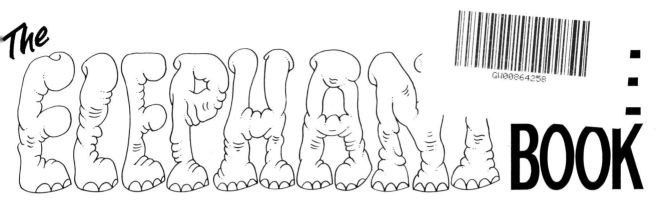

The ELEPHANT BOOK

Scoular Anderson

Hippo

Scholastic Children's Books
Scholastic Publications Ltd,
7-9 Pratt Street, London NW1 0AE

Scholastic Inc.,
730 Broadway, New York, NY 10003, USA

Scholastic Canada Ltd,
123 Newkirk Road, Richmond Hill,
Ontario L4C 3G5, Canada

Ashton Scholastic Pty Ltd,
PO Box 579, Gosford, New South Wales,
Australia

Ashton Scholastic Ltd,
Private Bag 1, Penrose, Auckland,
New Zealand.

First published by Scholastic Publications Ltd., 1993

Text and illustrations copyright © Scoular Anderson, 1993

ISBN: 0 590 55174 4

Typesetting by Rapid Reprographics, London

Printed and bound by The Paramount Printing Group Ltd.

Why are elephants so wrinkled?
Have you ever tried ironing one?

What do you call an
elephant that flies?
A jumbo jet.

Who is beautiful, grey and
wears glass slippers?
Cinderelephant.

How do elephants
climb trees?
They use their trunks.

5

What's bright red and weighs four tonnes?
An elephant holding its breath.

What's blue and has big ears?
An elephant at the North Pole.

What's grey, has big ears and is good with ice cream?
A jellyphant.

What's grey, has four legs
and a trunk?
A mouse going on holiday.

8

What's big, grey and scary?
An elephantom.

What do you call an elephant that's wearing a Walkman?
Anything. He can't hear you.

What is two feet long, has sixteen eyes and a big tongue?
An elephant's training shoe.

9

What's the difference between an elephant and a flea?
Elephants can have fleas but fleas can't have elephants.

What do you call an elephant in rubber boots?
A wellyphant.

What's the difference between an elephant and a gooseberry?
A gooseberry is green.

What do you get if you cross an elephant with a kangaroo?
Big holes all over Australia.

What do you do when an elephant sits in front of you at the cinema?

> *Miss most of the film.*

What's grey and wrinkly and jumps every thirty seconds?
An elephant with hiccups.

Why do elephants have wrinkly ankles?
Because their shoes are too tight.

How can you tell when there's an elephant in the back of your car?
You can smell the peanuts on its breath.

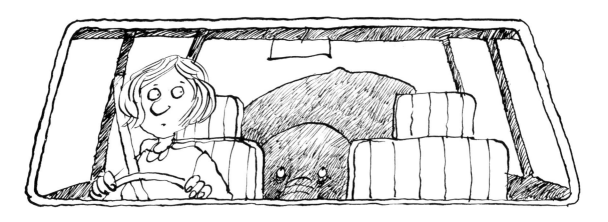

What's grey and wrinkly and has sixteen wheels?
An elephant on roller skates.

What's big, grey and flies straight up?

An elecopter

What's grey and wrinkly and has two wheels?
An elephant on a motorbike.

What game do elephants play in minis?
Squash.

What's the first thing to do when an elephant breaks its toe?
Call a toe truck.

What's the difference between an elephant and a banana?
Have you ever tried to peel an elephant?

What do you call an elephant
that can't do sums?
Dumbo.

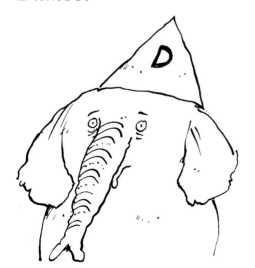

What do you call an elephant
that never washes?
A smellyphant.

Why do elephants wear sandals?

To stop them sinking into the sand

Why do ostriches stick their heads in the sand?

To look for the elephants that weren't wearing sandals!

Which is stronger, an elephant or a snail?
A snail, because it carries its house. An elephant only carries its trunk.

How can you spot an elephant in your gravy?
It's very, very lumpy!

Why do elephants never have dandruff?

Have you ever seen an elephant with long hair?

What's the best way to get a wild elephant?
Buy a tame one first then annoy it.

What's the difference between an elephant and a mouse?
A mouse makes smaller holes in the skirting board.

How can you tell the difference between an Indian elephant and an African elephant?
Look at their passports.

What do you do with old cannon balls?
Give them to elephants to use as marbles.

Why couldn't the two elephants go swimming?
They only had one pair of trunks.

Why do elephants have ivory tusks?
Because iron ones would rust.

What's the difference between an elephant and a digestive biscuit?
Have you ever tried dunking an elephant in your tea?

What do elephants do in the evenings?
Watch elevision.

How do you know if there's an elephant in your oven?
You can't shut the door.

How do you know if there's an elephant in your fridge?
Because of the footprints in the butter.

What's white on the outside, grey in the middle and heavy on the stomach?
An elephant sandwich.

What's grey, weighs four tonnes and goes clump, clump, swish, swish?
An elephant with slippers on its back feet.

What's big and grey and protects you from the rain?
An umbrellaphant.

Who lost a herd of
elephants?
Big Bo Peep.

Why can't elephants sing?
*Maybe they can but they don't
want to be mistaken for birds.*

How do animals greet each
other?

What do you call a mouse that can lift an elephant?
Sir!